Tabl

MW00413995

Contact the Author:

Tayvon Jackson

TayvonJackson123@gmail.com

240-423-5787

Introduction

I was born 28 years ago, one of the so many fatherless children born to a single Black mother. I sometimes wonder what my father would have said to me if we had ever reunited. I wonder how my life would have been different if I'd had my dad around. Would it have changed who I am, or how I see the world? I like to think that his absence made no difference in who I am and that I was born to be what I have become. I have been fortunate to have a great stepdad that I love and who has filled that role of the father in my life, but all a kid can do is wonder. What if?

As a child, I had the same fantasies about my real dad that most children in my circumstances do. My dad was an athlete, a businessman, a pilot, or a superhero, and someday he would come back to my mother and me and we would live happily ever after, probably in a big house with a huge yard and maybe even a dog. We would be a happy and complete family, just like the lucky kids at school, just like what I saw on TV. Of course, those dreams didn't come true. But not once have I ever used the absence of my real dad as an excuse.

There is an epidemic in the African American community. There are too many fatherless children, too many people struggling to survive, too much poverty, and a general attitude of dependency upon social welfare and charity. There is a lack of ambition, a loss of faith in our education system, and a lack of hope. Too many Black children are growing up thinking that the way they live now is as good as they can hope for. The media puts these unrealistic realities on our youth, highlighting the athletes and the rappers, instead of the doctors and engineers.

Beyond the general bleakness and acceptance of the circumstances, there is a lack of motivation to better ourselves. We are taught from childhood by society, to accept our fate, to not work and depend on charity, or to work for low pay at menial jobs. We are not surprised by crime, discrimination, or cruelty. We are not trying to change our circumstances. Of course, this does not apply to everyone, but unfortunately, it happens enough that this is a topic.

If only my peers can see the light at the end of the tunnel like I can. There is a way to uplift ourselves and our community. There is a way to give ourselves and our families a better life. There are resources that we have that will enable us, as a people, to do better than we currently are doing. We need to help each other, educate ourselves, and stop depending on the government to take care of us.

The success of a Black person should not be a rare and miraculous event. It should not be a story of some poor, disadvantaged child growing up to beat the odds. It should, instead, be something that we expect to happen. We should be teaching our children, through our example, that they are capable of doing anything they put their minds to.

I know that I can rise above where I began. I know that when I get to hold my newborn child in my arms, I will never leave their side.   I will be the best father ever!!! My No Dad was not in my life and as I checked the mail, I found a letter addressed to me from him. Should I rip it up, burn it, or read it; this couldn't be real.   I must be dreaming; I haven't heard from my dad since I was a young child. Afraid of what the letter would say, I knew that turning this letter into a book would help ease my worries and allow me to share with the world what my No Dad had to say.

I will do better than my father. I will be the father that I wanted to have. I will be there to guide my children through life. I will be the dad that is an example for my children.

My presence will be more than just a hastily scribbled letter. But the only question I had was how did it get here without a stamp?????

The Letter

Dear Son,

The night you were born was the happiest of my life. Despite the anxiety I felt, and the nerves leading up to your birth, I had concerns about how I was going to raise a son in this complicated world. The moment you were placed in my arms I was the proudest person on Earth. There is something awesome about seeing your child for the first time, hearing those first life-affirming cries from a tiny human being that has your blood in his veins. My son! I wanted, I still want, to give you the world. I want to give you everything, all the comforts and material things that would make your life comfortable and soft. I want you to grow without worry, without stress, without a struggle. I want you to grow into a successful, confident man that never knows the agony of doing without, a man who has never known hardship and loss and never will.

However, I realize that I cannot give you that life. As I stood in that sterile, dark hospital room, staring at you in that bassinet, your entire life was stretching out in front of you. I knew I could not give you the carefree life of leisure that I envisioned. I knew, even in that wondrous cloud of new fatherhood, that even if I could give you that kind of life, I shouldn't give you everything. All I can give you is advice from your poor dad; knowledge acquired from my own life of struggle. My own battles with poverty and a world that I thought was keeping me down in the guts of humanity, chained to being dependent on other people's charity, trapped in a cycle of hard work that never paid off, relying on the government to keep me fed and housed and employed.

Son! You have to know how hard it was for me when you were growing up. I know there were times you wanted things I couldn't give you- fancy shoes, a new bicycle, things you saw on TV, things your spoiled classmates had. I know there were times you hated the substandard housing project we lived in, I know there were times you hated me for not having the means to give you the things you wanted. You watched me work long hours at a low paying job, coming home bone tired to a tiny house with scratched floors and sagging ceilings. At times, there were hard words between us, especially when I wanted you to do better than I had done.

There were times, too, when I knew you were proud to

have a father around, when so many of your friends didn't. I was proud of you; I wouldn't have missed watching you grow up for anything. I couldn't always be there in the ways I wanted to be, but you grew up into a fine young man. I watch you now, from afar, on the brink of leaving home, starting your own life's journey. That's why I wanted to write all this down for you, to remind you of how amazing you are, to give you a guide so that you don't make my mistakes.

Some of us poor dads think that the only way to achieve anything in life is to get a good education, to get a good job after you've finished that education. I admit that there were times I thought that way, too. I would look at you while you slept; a little boy that was so full of talent and potential, and believe that one fine day, my little boy would be a lawyer or doctor or great scientist; my beautiful son would grow up to be more than I was, know more than me, go to places I'd never seen. I worried about how I would pay for you to go to college, or worry that you have to get loans to go to school, graduating with debt you'd be paying on for years. As the value of a degree is sinking even as tuition gets higher.

Chapter 1: Poor Dad – No Dad

Son, I have felt crippled by poverty, by a feeling that I can't get past what I am- a Black man. I let myself be deceived by my upbringing, that the only way of life was what I knew. I grew up in a broken, crumbling housing projects with a single mother and I never met my father. Maybe this was the reason why I didn't stick around. This is a great sadness to me, to our community. There are those, sadly, within our race who know this is just the way things are, that we can't get past it, as this is part of our culture, a "ghetto culture." Some people will say that we, as African Americans, are held back from greatness by the White man. Son! Get this thinking out of your head.

Black people have allowed the government to take care of them, cursing the world that keeps them dependent on government assistance. A race that began in this country as slaves had in a sense, never left the plantation. Such a large percentage of us never try to move beyond letting others take care of us, still telling us how much food we can have, where we can live, and what work we can do. Many of us are so worried about getting our forty acres and a mule that we don't strive to create dividends. These are not restrictions the White population has put on us. These are restrictions we put on ourselves by not trying to rise above our current circumstances. These are chains of our making, by saying that it is our culture to have fatherless children, living in despair, dependent on society to take care of us. Son!! Do not think like this.

Chapter 2: How to Hustle and Win

When I say you have to hustle, I'm not telling you to live on social welfare and deal in illegal activities to get ready cash in your pocket. That's the kind of behavior that keeps the African American community dependent on charity. Social welfare is charity, and it has its place, but its place should not be to support the majority of a race. There may be less stress involved in getting your house and food provided for you, but what kind of man does that make you, when you are dependent upon someone else to pay for you to have the basics you need to survive? Are you still on that plantation, waiting for the overseer to hand you your meal? Make your bread or buy your bread.

The hustler I'm telling you to be is a survivor. A man that works for what he has, who uses the skills and resources available to him to make a living, to make a life, to make himself into a man he can be proud of. Have more pride in yourself than to stand merely in line, waiting for a handout from other people's labor. You already have all the skills you need to succeed. I taught you all you need to know, all the things your poor dad learned the hard way, from a hard life.

Help Others

You may be saying you can't assist others because you have nothing to give. You are wrong, son, you have plenty to give that can be your smile, your time, your kindness, honesty, patience, compassion and your encouraging words. If you want to succeed, you must recognize the value in other people. Everyone has hard times, issues that they have to overcome. I'm not telling you to shoulder their burdens for them but I'm saying you must not add more weight to their troubles.

You do not want to be the type of man that gains his success from misleading people. That kind of success is short-lived, and can mark you forever as someone who isn't to be trusted. I wouldn't want my son marked as a fraud, not when you could be a real hustler, a real businessman.

Hustling is not about being deceitful, or using other people for your gain. What kind of man do you want to be? A respected man is not one who lies, or cheats, or steals to get ahead, but a guy who embraces challenges overcomes adversity while still holding on to his integrity. A respected man is a man who gives back to humanity. If you want to be the guy that is respected and admired, you must be worthy of it.

Be Yourself

You have been told all your life that if you want people to like you, just be yourself. This is still true. If you are living a lie, even a lie to yourself, you are not gaining anything. As I always say, keep it real. Be true to yourself, and always respect yourself. Don't follow the crowd just to gain popularity. Who cares about popularity, if it's not who you are?

If you are not authentic, it will show in everything you do. You can't make real friends; you can't be a true friend if you are not genuine. How are you going to find a nice girl and settle down if that nice girl doesn't know the real you? The boy I raised is good enough for anybody if you'll just remember to let your real self out.

Have True Friends

As a child, you needed friends to play with, to develop socially, to play Power Rangers, and to moan about homework with. As you grew, you needed friends to talk to about girls, go to school functions with, play sports and imagine with. You always knew who your real friends were, the ones that wanted the best for you, the ones that could keep your secrets and were willing to listen to your problems. I know that you know how

12

to be a good friend. I've watched you grow from a helpless infant to the fine young man you are today, even from afar and I know you are a friend to be proud of.

You will need friends at every stage of your life, from all different walks of life, from every background. You need these friends to keep you in check, to keep you grounded, to listen to you, to help you through the rough patches that you will, inevitably and regretfully, have to face.

Ask for Help
Don't be too proud to ask for help. There's a difference between a handout and a hand up. Do you want to go to college? Talk to your teachers, look at scholarship options, study hard, and get that diploma. Do you want to build houses, fix cars, play ball, travel the world? I don't care what you chose but find a mentor that can set you on the path to achieving your dreams. I am sorry that I couldn't be that mentor for you. Educate yourself and take advantage of every opportunity the world gives you.

You may think that the color of your skin will prevent people from helping you to succeed. You never know until you ask. Sure, some people may not want to show you the tricks of their trade, but others will be more than willing to help. Keep asking until you find the mentor you need. Then work hard, add value, and prove that you are worthy of their time because you are.

Failure is Good

Don't be afraid to fail. You will learn from your mistakes. If you don't succeed the first time you try, look at what went wrong and try again. You can't go through life afraid of failure. If you dwell on that fear, it will hold you back from success. Look at every failed attempt as just as an attempt. Success comes to those who aren't afraid to make mistakes. Each mistake you make gets you one step closer to what you want because you have learned what doesn't work.

Focus

Do not let anything distract you. Turn off your phone sometimes; shut down the TV and stop worrying about how many "likes" you have on Facegram and Instabook or whatever they're called. Live in the present, live in the real world. Too many people are living in poverty, worried about how many followers they have instead of thinking of ways to get out their situation.

What do you want the most? Follow your heart, follow your dreams. If anything is distracting you from providing for yourself and your family, you need to cut it out of your life. It doesn't matter how many virtual friends think you're the man. You need to be the man in real life, in real time.

Never Stop

Never relax. Don't think that just because you're comfortable now that you will always be comfortable. Always look for ways to improve; there is always room for improvement. There is always another opportunity to work harder, to expand your mind, to seek a higher meaning. As the saying goes, there is always another mountain to climb. Keep climbing those mountains keep on reaching for the sky. There is never a limit to success and there is never a point that can't be passed.

You may think that you don't have to prove yourself anymore, but you're wrong. Hustling is all about proving yourself every single day. You have to prove that you can do it, that you can succeed. Then, you have to prove that you can keep up the momentum, that you can keep being successful. You don't have to prove it to me, or to the world, but to yourself. Once you have found success, you will keep hustling because it is who you are.

Chapter 3: Watch Your Money

I have struggled with debt. It is a weight I would never want you to have to carry. It's tempting to take out a small payday loan or juggle a few credit cards. It may seem harmless, but it can turn into a vicious cycle of debt, having to borrow from one creditor to pay another. Be careful anytime you are considering going into debt. The last thing I want for you is to see you back on that plantation because of debt.

Unexpected expenses come up in life; hospital bills, car repairs, home repairs, and temporary unemployment. Put some money away for life's emergencies. Don't just slap down the plastic to pay for it. There may be a better way to pay for things that you need. Having some emergency cash can be a real lifesaver.

Make sure you invest son. The value of your money is going down every day that you don't. Take the time to learn about stocks, real estate, and build wealth. But don't be a selfish son; the seeds you plant today will leave a legacy for many generations after you. You always were good with numbers, maybe you will grow up and be a stock trader on Wall Street.

Have a Plan

You have to have a plan if you are going to get ahead in life. It doesn't matter what you want to do. You have to have a strategy in place to get where you're going. When you fail to plan, you plan to fail. You wouldn't drive across the country without a map, or directions to get where you're going. The same is true in life. Figure out where it is you want to go, and then figure out how you're going to get there.

Imagine you are a soldier, and your success is a war to be won. How do you plan each battle, each move, to lead yourself through each and every campaign, until the war is won? It is okay to fall back sometimes, evaluate your situation, gather more resources, and then go forward. Just keep in mind, to win the war; you have to keep moving forward.

Avoid Balance Transfers

There are times you may save money by transferring the balance of one card to another, such as transferring to a lower interest card. That's a smart move *if* you cut up the high-interest card. If you are only transferring debt to clear up credit on another card, you are just adding to bad debt. Be smart, son, and watch the debt you are building.

Pay On Time and In Full

You should pay those credit cards off every single month, and pay them off on time. You will not only have more credit available in the event of an emergency. You won't be stressed out over high-interest building over time, or damage your credit with late notices and fees.

Only Charge What You Can Afford

If you can't afford an item, it can be tempting just to charge it and tell yourself you can just make payments. Son, if you can't afford something, you have just to live without it. You don't want to get into the habit of charging things. Live within your means, and avoid running yourself deep into debt for items you can't afford. If you can't pay cash for something, don't charge it.

Never Charge Disposable Items

You should not use credit cards to pay for things that will be gone when the credit card bill arrives. Don't use those cards to pay for groceries or restaurants. These items can add up quickly because you have a higher spending limit on a credit card than if you were paying cash. You could be tempted to buy more because you can, and not think about the debt you incur, not just from the items you charged, but the interest that accumulates.

Use Cash Advances Only in Emergencies

Using your credit card to get a cash advance is the fastest way to build up bad debt. If you find yourself using your cards for getting cash, you need to take a big step back and consider your situation. Why are you relying on these advances? You need to evaluate what you are spending this money on and take a better hold on your finances, or your finances will control you.

There may be emergencies where a cash advance is unavoidable and necessary. Even in that situation, you need to consider what you are paying for that money. Factor in the interest rate and how hard it will be to get that advance paid for.

Your Credit Cards Are Yours

Your credit cards are just that- yours. Don't let other people use your cards and run up debt you have to pay for. Once your credit cards are out of your control, you have no say in how they are being used. Do not let your good heart override your good sense. You need to stay in charge of your finances, and that means staying in charge of your credit cards.

Understand Your Credit Card Terms

You need to educate yourself on interest rates as well as fully understand the terms on your credit card. After all, these rates and terms affect your finances. If the interest rates are high, you are paying a lot more for what you charge. Never agree to a credit card that is ultimately going to cause more harm than good to your financial situation.

Don't Have Too Many Credit Cards

One or two credit cards are fine, perhaps even necessary, to maintain a good credit score, or for travel or other things that may require using a credit card. Just don't let yourself become dependent on those cards. Remember, the more plastic in your wallet, the more debt you can accumulate. Use cash whenever possible, and always avoid debt when you can.

Chapter 4: Mind Your Own Business

We live in a world where people believe in showing off what they have and getting involved in things that don't concern them. Social media can be damaging to your self-esteem, especially if you are wasting time wishing you had what other people have, or if you let yourself get pulled into silly dramas that don't have anything to do with you or your situation. Focus on what you are striving for. Mind your own business and let other people mind theirs. It is up to you to make your life, so never let outside influences determine the manner with which you do so. Letting yourself get involved or concerned with what other people are doing is a good way to get yourself off track from your goals. If you want to make it through life, son, keep your mind on your matters and not on other people's business.

Chapter 5: Tips for Success

Success means a lot of different things to different people. Everyone has his or her definition of what it's like to make it in life. You have to figure out what success means to you and go for it.

It doesn't matter that you are starting your journey from humble beginnings. It's up to you to make the most of what you have and start working on achieving what you want. Your background can be a handicap or an asset; the distinction is ultimately up to you. As your father, perhaps I am biased, but I know my boy has what it takes to do anything you want to do. Just keep these tips in mind and you'll go far.

Dream Big

Never settle for being acceptable in life, always strive to be the very best. Make goals that seem impossible and keep reaching for them. You don't want ever to let yourself think that good is good enough. You have to keep reaching higher and higher, never allowing yourself to become lazy and complacent. Dream big dreams and keep striving to achieve them.

Do What You Love

If you want to be truly successful, you have to be passionate about what you do, not just the money you make. If you love what you do, you will not measure success by money, but with achievement. The secret to being fulfilled by what you do is to have genuinely a love for the career you choose. You won't mind long hours or the little disappointments as much, if you enjoy your work.

Maintain Balance

There is a delicate balance between your work life and your home life. You have to find a way to make both a priority so that you have a full, balanced life. There will be times when one requires more of your time than the other. Yes, you can go out sometimes and have fun and travel but focus on what is important. That's just how life goes. Make sure you know how important it is, not only to be successful at work but to be successful in your home life, as well.

Failure is a Good Thing

If you are afraid of failure, you are also afraid of success. You can't expect to succeed at everything on the first try. Learn to accept failure not as a defeat but as an opportunity. You must crawl before you walk.

You will fail more than once, so start to view every wrong turn as a chance to improve your game.

Control Your Destiny

You'll never get off the plantation by standing still. Don't sit around waiting for things to happen- make them happen for you. If you want to be your own man, you have to take full responsibility for your life instead of letting other people make those decisions for you. Stand up and start moving forward with your power so that when you do succeed, you can take full credit for your achievements.

Work Well With Others

If you want to have a full, successful life, you have to get along with other people. You are not the only person in the world with feelings, thoughts, or opinions. Starting first is a waste of time and energy. There will be times you need help or advice, and you will need to have a positive relationship with people for this. Treat others the way you want to be treated. You'll be a better man.

Share Your Ideas

Your thoughts have merit. Never be afraid to share your mind with other people. Successful people are not afraid to take risks with their thoughts, and you shouldn't be, either. When you have the opportunity to bounce your ideas off of other people, benefit from it! You should never let fear stand in the way of your thoughts.

Think Positive

Stay positive! No matter how bad things may seem, having a bad attitude will only make things worse- and make you miserable in the process. Learn always to look on the bright side, and never forget how blessed you are.

Trust Your Gut

You know the difference between right and wrong. You know what the right decision is for you. There will be times that other people will try to steer you away from what you are doing. They will attempt to persuade you to do what they think is right, even when you know it isn't the right choice for you.

Listen to your gut; listen to your heart, before you follow the crowd. If you know, deep down, that something is right, why let someone else's opinion steer you off course? Your real friends will respect you for following your instincts. Anyone who doesn't is not your friend.

Chapter 6: When the Going Gets Tough, the Tough Get Going

L ife can be difficult, hard, and disappointing. You will have tough times to deal with- financially, physically, and emotionally. There will be times you can't see past the rough spot you're in. Don't fall into despair, don't be tempted to throw in the towel and quit. Keep your head up, son.

Life is short, life is precious, and life matters. I don't want you ever to forget that. You have to look at every challenge you're faced with as an opportunity to learn, to prevail, to survive. Use your brain; use all the resources available to you to overcome the hard times. Never give up, no matter the odds. You can do anything you put your mind to.

Chapter 7: Start Moving

It's up to you to get the ball rolling on your success. If you want to reach the top, you can't sit there making excuses. You are never too young or too old to make your life better. If you want something, you have to make it happen. Success is not something you just wake up to; it isn't something you can buy or have given to you. If you want to be successful, you have to start making steps towards it on your own.

Once you figure out what you want, make a list. Know your weaknesses as well as your strengths. You do have some bad qualities, son, but you also have plenty of good qualities to balance it out. Work on improving the bad as well as the good, and, most importantly, keep moving toward your goals.

Chapter 8: Act Like a Hustler

If you want to be a first class hustler, act like one! A real enthusiast isn't sitting on his backside watching TV all day, or hanging out with his buddies every weekend turning up at the club. A hustler is a businessman and businessmen spend their time doing business, not wasting time on trivial matters. Son, I want you to pay attention to how successful people behave. Those are the habits you need to adopt for yourself.

Chapter 9: Stay On Track

Once you make your plan, you have to stick to it. There are plenty of distractions, lots of things that will come up that can take your head out of the game. Keep your eyes on the prize, son, instead of on the sidelines. Before you let yourself be distracted by the inconsequential, ask yourself: "Will this help me succeed?" If the answer is "no" , then you need to ask yourself why you are letting yourself be distracted!

Some things are worth your time, and things that aren't. Learn to tell the difference. If you are spending time on things that aren't helping you to become a success, you are making a mistake that will be hard to go right. Stay on course, son, and you'll get where you need and want to be.

Chapter 10: Rise Above Your Circumstances

You are coming from a hard place, son, and you will have to work hard to succeed. You may think your background will hold you back and that being a poor Black kid will determine how you live for the rest of your life. You're wrong, son! You will have to work, and work hard, but you can rise above your beginnings. It may be easier to sit back and let other people take care of you, but how will you hold your head up, how can you be a man worthy of respect, if you accept charity? Why should you feel that you shouldn't have to work hard? The first thing you must realize is that the world owes you nothing; if you want to rise above where you are, you must work to get there.

Chapter 11: Being a Positive Influence

Life is short, far too short, to allow yourself to be negative. Enjoy life, take the time to notice and appreciate the good things around you. Be a positive influence to those you come in contact with. Your thoughts influence your actions, so make sure you are acting for good and not letting yourself become a shallow, empty person.

Don't ever forget that it is up to you to fill your life with positive things. If you allow yourself to be surrounded by negative people, you will find yourself taking on their thoughts and actions. Take the time to make positive connections with people that can influence you for good, not people that drag you down.

Pay attention to your thoughts and actions. You want to be a positive force in the world. Someday you will be a role model for your children. Be the man you would want your son to be. Act like the man you would want your daughter to marry. When you think about how you impact those you love, it makes you want to be a better man. When you think about how short life is, you will understand how little time you have to make an impression.

Chapter 12:Stay on Budget

Always live within your means. It can be so tempting when you have cash in your hand or a green credit card, to buy what you want without thinking about what you need. It can seem like no big deal, just a few little purchases here and there. You've got to set a budget and stick to it. I'm not telling you to deprive yourself of ever buying frivolous things. I'm saying you need to budget and budget well son. Take care of the essentials first, put money back for emergencies, then think about the things you want.

Conclusion

Son, there are so many things that you have to offer the world. You are smart, creative, and, most of all, you are compassionate, caring, and kind. I can only hope that you will use those skills to take yourself farther in life.

You will have hurdles that you must propel yourself over. You will have to apply yourself harder to get past the circumstances you are currently in. You will have to take charge of your life and keep your eyes on the prize if you want to have more in life. Son, I have no doubt that you will make it.

Take control of your finances early in life, always know the value of a dollar and never be afraid to work hard. There is no shame in an honest day's work for an honest day's pay. There *is* a shame, however, in an able-bodied man sitting back, waiting for a handout. Do not fall into the trap of expecting others to provide for you. If you want to be independent, you must learn only to depend on yourself for what you need. The world doesn't owe you a thing, and you'll be a better person if you remember that. You have to hustle if you want to succeed in life.

You were born with everything you need to survive in life. You have your two hands, two legs, your sharp mind, a good heart, and a strong mother who would do anything for you. You're all set for success. You will be able to find ways to excel in business, in life. You won't merely survive, son; I know you'll thrive. You have the skills you were born with, the rest you will learn as you go along.

Take every opportunity to educate yourself along the way. You should never assume you know all you need to know. There are plenty of ways to keep learning throughout your life. Take advantage of them. Part of winning at life is being able to open your mind, to let yourself absorb all the knowledge you can. Nothing you learn is ever wasted. Remember that!

Know who your friends are, and be faithful to those friends. When you meet a good girl, treat her right. Don't ever abandon the people that love you. Learn the difference between people that love you and people that are using you. Never take advantage of people's affections. In all things, be honest and hold on to your integrity.

I leave this for you in hopes that you will be the better man. I hope that you will be stronger, smarter, and more determined than I have been. I know that when you are standing in my place, years from now, you will not slip out of your child's life as a coward. I understand, son, that you may hate me for leaving you and your mother. Right now, I hate myself, too. I only know that I cannot be the father you need. My fear of failure is preventing me from trying.

Do not make my mistakes. Be stronger, and braver, than I have been. Take charge of your destiny, and don't let anything hold you back.

Love Always,

Your Dad

Closing

I awoke in a cold sweat to my alarm clock ringing. This amazing letter that taught me everything I needed to know about life, money, and everything else had only been a dream. There was never any letter, still no dad, but just fruitful thoughts in a young boy's mind. Disappointed, I woke up with a sense of motivation and a whole new outlook on life. I could accomplish anything that I wanted to and there was no one that could stop me. I never had a dream so clear and so concise in my life but I believe the lessons I envisioned should be shared with the world. Not everyone had a Rich Dad growing up; in fact some people had No Dad at all. Take control of your situation, stop making excuses, and use my dream, my No Dad's letter, as a foundation to accomplish everything that you want in life.

TO BE CONTINUED......

Contact the Author:

Tayvon Jackson

TayvonJackson123@gmail.com
240-423-5787